Lanterns in the Dark

Lanterns In the Dark

Stories of Survival, Scars, and Light

Lanterns in the Dark

*"One friend, one person who is truly understanding,
who takes the trouble to listen to us as we consider our
problems, can change our whole outlook on the world."*

-Elisabeth Kübler-R

Lanterns in the Dark

Table of Contents

Lanterns in the Dark

*"When I realized the storm
was inevitable, I made it
my medicine."*
-Andrea Gib

Lanterns in the Dark

INTRODUCTION
BY BETSY CHASSE

There are stories we tell easily.

Stories about our work, our families, the places we have traveled, and the things that make us laugh. These stories move freely through conversations. They are shared around dinner tables, across coffee cups, and in passing moments with friends and strangers.

And then there are the other stories.

The ones that live quietly beneath the surface. The ones we hesitate to name out loud. These are the moments that changed us in ways we did not expect. Moments that left marks we carry long after the world has moved on.

Most of us hold those stories carefully. Sometimes we guard them with silence. Sometimes we release pieces of them when the weight becomes too heavy to carry alone. And sometimes we share them without quite knowing why, only sensing that something inside us needs to be witnessed.

Trauma does not come with instructions.

No one teaches us exactly how to hold pain, how to speak about it, or how to respond when someone else places their story in our hands. Instead, we learn slowly through experience. Through trial, through missteps, and through moments of unexpected understanding.

Many people respond to pain by speaking often and openly about it. They tell their story in different rooms, to different listeners, hoping that somewhere along the way someone will truly understand. There can be relief in naming what happened. Words can feel like air entering a space that has long been closed.

Others move in the opposite direction. They carry their experiences quietly, believing that silence is safer. They may worry that their story will make others uncomfortable, or that it will be misunderstood. Sometimes the silence grows so familiar that speaking feels impossible.

Most of us move between these two spaces throughout our lives. There are moments when we speak too much and moments when we say nothing at all.

At the center of both responses is the same human longing.

We want to be understood.

Yet understanding requires something that our culture often struggles to practice. It requires listening without rushing to change what we hear.

When someone shares a painful experience, our instincts tend to move quickly. We offer advice. We try to solve the problem. We search for hopeful lessons or reassuring explanations. We may even share our own stories in an attempt to connect.

These responses usually come from care. We want to help. We want to ease the discomfort of watching another person suffer.

But sometimes the most meaningful response is also the simplest.

To listen.

To allow someone to tell the truth of their experience without interruption, correction, or judgment. To let their words exist exactly as they are spoken.

There is a particular kind of healing that happens in the presence of a listener who does not try to reshape the story.

Being witnessed can change the way we carry our past.

It does not erase what happened. It does not undo the pain or rewrite the moment. But it does something important. It reminds us that our experiences are real and that they matter.

This book was created with that understanding in mind.

The writers in these pages have each chosen to share a moment from their lives that left a mark. These are not stories written to prove that everything has been resolved or perfectly healed. Life rarely offers such clean endings.

Instead, these essays are acts of honesty.

Each author has stepped forward and said, in their own voice, this is something that happened to me. This is how it shaped me. This is how I continue to live with what I experienced.

Some stories may carry grief. Others may reveal quiet resilience. Some may leave questions that have not yet found answers.

That is part of what makes them meaningful.

Real life is rarely tidy. It moves through uncertainty, contradiction, and growth that unfolds slowly over time. By allowing these stories to remain authentic rather than polished into simple lessons, the writers invite readers into a more honest kind of connection.

These pages are not about rescuing anyone from their past.

They are about witnessing it.

When we witness someone else's truth, something subtle begins to happen within us.

The distance between our lives becomes smaller. Experiences that once felt isolating begin to feel more familiar.

A sentence in someone else's story might remind us of a moment from our own life. A reflection might echo a feeling we have carried quietly for years. A stranger's words might reveal something we have struggled to put into language.

In those moments, we begin to recognize an important truth.

Our stories may be unique, but the emotions that live within them are deeply human and widely shared.

Grief, fear, courage, loss, survival, hope. These experiences move quietly through many lives, even when they are not spoken aloud.

Storytelling has always been one of the ways human beings find one another through those shared emotions. Long before books, people gathered around fires and spoke about what they had lived through. Those stories carried warnings, wisdom, comfort, and companionship.

They reminded listeners that someone else had walked through something difficult and survived.

In many ways, this book continues that ancient tradition.

Each essay is a voice speaking from lived experience. Each voice adds another perspective on what it means to endure hardship, to grow through it, and to keep moving forward with honesty.

For the writers who contributed to this collection, telling these stories required courage. It is not easy to revisit moments that changed us or to place those experiences before an audience of readers.

Yet courage often begins in quiet ways.

It begins with a decision to speak truthfully.

And when one person chooses honesty, it often opens a door for others to do the same.

A single story can create recognition. It can offer language to someone who has struggled to describe their own experiences. It can bring comfort to a reader who believes their feelings are theirs alone.

Stories have the power to reach across distance and remind us that connection is possible, even between strangers.

As you move through this collection, you are invited to take on an important role.

You are the witness.

You are the person sitting with these writers as they share pieces of their lives. You are the presence that receives their stories and holds them with care.

You do not need to solve anything within these pages. You do not need to search for perfect answers or clear conclusions.

Your role is simply to listen.

Allow each voice to speak. Allow each story to unfold at its own pace. Allow yourself to feel whatever responses arise as you read.

In doing so, you participate in something quietly powerful.

You create space for truth.

And within that space, something meaningful often begins to grow. Understanding deepens. Compassion expands. The distance between our lives becomes smaller.

This is how stories do their work in the world.

They remind us that survival takes many forms. They show us that scars can exist alongside strength. They reveal that healing is not always a single moment but often a long and complicated journey.

Most importantly, they remind us that no one walks through darkness entirely alone.

The title of this book reflects that idea.

A lantern does not erase the night. It does not remove every shadow or obstacle along the path. What it offers is something quieter but just as powerful.

A lantern offers light.

It reveals enough of the path for the next step to be taken. It allows those who are walking nearby to recognize one another. It reminds travelers that even in the deepest darkness, illumination is possible.

The stories in this book are lanterns carried by the people who lived them.

Each writer has lifted their own light and placed it here for others to see. Their stories do not claim perfection or certainty. They simply offer honesty, reflection, and the courage to speak about experiences that shaped their lives.

Together, these voices create a gathering of lights.

And when many lanterns are lifted at once, the darkness begins to change. What once felt isolating begins to feel shared. What once felt silent begins to feel understood.

This book is that gathering.

A collection of voices.

A record of survival.

A reminder that even our scars can illuminate the way for someone else.

As you begin reading, you are invited to slow down and be present with each story you encounter.

Listen carefully.

Somewhere within these pages, you may recognize a piece of your own journey. You may find words for feelings you have carried quietly. You may discover that another person has walked a path that feels strikingly familiar.

And perhaps, by the time you reach the final page, you will see what these writers already know.

Even in the darkest moments of human experience, there are lights being raised.

Story by story.

Voice by voice.

Lantern by lantern.

Welcome to Lanterns in the Dark.

About Betsy Chasse

Betsy Chasse is an award-winning filmmaker, best-selling author, publisher, and, most importantly, a mom. She is best known as the co-creator of the groundbreaking film *What the Bleep Do We Know?!* and has directed and produced several documentaries, including *Song of the New Earth*, *Pregnant in America*, and *The Empty Womb*.

She is the author of multiple books, including *Killing Buddha*, *Tipping Sacred Cows*, and *The Documentary Filmmaking Master Class*, as well as other works exploring consciousness, culture, and the contradictions of being human.

Betsy also writes a bold and often sassy Substack where she explores the paradoxes of modern life, tipping over a few sacred cows along the way and inviting readers into deeper conversations about truth, belief, and what it means to be human.

1

ON THE NATURE OF LETTING GO
BY HEIDI ZIN

I have always loved the inner life, and the mystical caught my attention. The practice of journeying with shamanism is a passion of interest, as was my art-making pursuits.

These decisions were not always supported by those in my life. They wanted me to choose a path they understood, one that fit their view of society, something deemed safer and more secure. I struggled to feel heard, to be seen, and understood.

I struggled in finding love for myself, to let my own little light shine forth. The skin I was being asked to wear was too tight and covered in shame. I was in the conditioning of the juvenile feminine. Trained to be pretty, polite, and pleasing, putting others' needs before my own.

I would wear this skin for decades, hiding, pretending "that's just the way it is".

This is what society was telling me how to fit in. This is what it wanted from me, this is how I could belong. Pushing the real self aside to fit the mold, I didn't fit the prescribed mold; it irritated me. I hated myself for trying to contort, to fit into a place that screamed NO within. I was in a struggle to find a place where the real me could use my voice, and I rebelled.

With talent already in place, my first struggle was not being recognized as the artist I wanted to be. Looking for opportunities, having the door shut in my face, and lacking the self-confidence to keep going. Difficulties in relationships, the loss of love, divorce, loneliness, and a near-death accident stripping me to the bare bones. I was being asked to rebuild a new life, and I was lost without a map.

I made decisions in life, not always in my best interest. I was caught up in distractions and chaos, trying to make things right. It took decades to find out who I really was, and it took a lot of adversity; it was often driven by dislikes, and it did not lead me in the direction my soul wanted to go.

I had a teacher-mentor in shamanism named Hank Wesselman. He had a mentor, a Hawaiian Kahuna Elder named Hale Makua. They told me this is the hardest planet, with the most daunting challenges. They stated that when we reach the other side, other beings meet us and exclaim, "You're an Earthling? Wow, (with reverence) tell us about it". They taught me that we learn from life's negative experiences, molding ourselves into stronger, more resilient vessels if we step up to the challenge.

This has definitely been true in my life. I have learned from those negative experiences. Trauma can be an amazing transformational tool if you allow it.

I have had many adversities and many challenges in life, and through them I have grown exponentially into who I always kind of knew I was inside, if I could just clear the brush away. Get out of my own way. This itself has been a struggle; there's no easy way to do it. We have to learn how to be a brave inner Soldier.

I often saw how others got through their trials as glimmers of hope, a feeling of, "I'm not alone; I'm not the only one with embarrassing failures." Oh no, I'm not that bad off, or "if she can, I can". On letting loss be my guide, "well, I'm not doing that again".

In 2011, I experienced one of the most traumatic events of my life. I struggled in love relationships. I struggled with my chosen family to be seen, heard, and taken seriously. On that day, I was trying to mend a relationship between myself, a man, and our young son. For all practical purposes, I was raising our child on my own. I felt it was up to me to pull us all together, and I felt alone in this.

On that day, we were taking a school trip across the ocean to an island for the 5th graders to pick an invasive weed. It was a very stormy, cold day, and we shouldn't have been out on the rough waters, so rough that we could not dock on the island when we arrived. We had to find another place to save this trip for the children. We did find another Island. Many of us wanted to go home, but it was not up to us.

On this smaller Island, the guide said we were looking for a tide pool, and we had to traverse over rocky cliffs, which we did successfully.

When we got to the other side of the bird poop-covered island, there were no tide pools that we could see. The tour guide said, "I think they're over that cliff". We looked at a 7-ft cliff beside the shoreline, with large boulders scattered about. He had hoisted all the children up over this cliff, and now they were out of sight. It was my turn.

He clearly was agitated and not paying attention. As I lifted my foot into his hands to give myself a boost, I let go of anything for support, and with a shove, he flung me up through the air. I knew there were boulders below me, and I was headed straight toward these boulders, headfirst.

Finding myself now somersaulting through the air, in that second, I had to face my death. I was going to die. I went through my realization. I made some sort of peace within myself with my inevitable ending. I knew this was not good. Time Stood Still, real still. The color separated out in a glow about me. I left my body, and then a loud CRACK, as my head hit the boulders first, then the rest of me. My lights Went Out.

I did not die. Upon coming to, I was unable to move, think, respond, or speak. I was not in my body; I was pushed way out. Others scrambled around me, trying to figure out what to do. The boat company had no idea, no first aid. It was a frenzy of activity, with many wrong decisions made, none of them on my part. Hours later, in shock, wet and cold, in severe pain, I was taken to the hospital.

Hearing gasps, I knew it was bad. My head wound was stapled back together. This took several hours. I was giddy with morphine and very happy to be alive.

But I was not prepared for what was to come next. With every organ in my body bruised and compromised, and having moved a quarter of an inch. With short-term memory loss, a jaw that was out of alignment, an eye that was compromised, an immobile neck, an inability to walk, and every inch of me in agonizing pain, I had to now learn to navigate my life back to working condition. I had to find my voice for my own healing.

This would take 10 plus years, and then some. Doctors and physical therapy became the norm. I had to learn to put myself first. I struggled to find Doctors with compassion, understanding, and support. Doctors who would take me without medical insurance. The trauma of poverty is a real thing, faced with denial where others treat you less than.

One of the things that hurt the most was that I did not expect, I struggled with feeling pushed out from the life I had before. The people that I had counted on, from the family I had created. They were not, could not, be there for me.

They were invested in keeping me the way I had been. The me who had been doing most of the navigation, the one smoothing things over or not needing attention, acquiescing to the desires of others. They wanted me, it seemed, to be as I once was, before the accident. Everything I knew was to fall away, bit by little bit, as I learned to navigate from a new place.

It was very difficult for my heartstrings to understand; it hurt, as they spoke behind my back. I was alone. Irritation and hurt were the only outlets, turned inward as I faced betrayal.

I finally let go when I realized no one I had counted on was there for me. When I finally stopped grasping at the old. Another free fall happened, this one emotionally. I finally started to let go of an old structure that had defined what life had been. I began an inner journey of healing.

I found that new life was waiting for me, but I had to find it. I had to struggle within myself to search for it.

My old life had stopped reaching out for me, and I watched it slowly dissolve. Hours and days of grief and crying helped me to wash away the distress and the sorrow and to finally see the value in myself and choose myself first, as this was all that was left remaining.

Watching sad movies helped the tears to flow, touching and opening my emotional body. Like the element of water, I was being washed clean. Like a dried tree being slowly watered, coming back to life. I began to see how deeply the *self* had been compromised. I wanted the pain I felt to become the presence and power that I knew was within that had not been recognized or acknowledged.

I learned I had been seeking solace and approval in a place that held shallowness for me. When I in truth, really desired depth, the depth that comes from an inner source, I was that depth. I began to turn towards myself through these traumatic events.

I learned that people can look at you and say, "Wow, you made it," and that it's an inspiration in the dark. Yet it's almost impossible for them to really understand, because they didn't have the same experience. You have gained confidence. The confidence of having made the journey shines forth anew. It reminds me of the story of the hobbits, returning to the Shire. Knowing that nobody could really relate to what they had experienced. It was theirs alone to hold as they reentered their community, but they knew they had been on their own Hero's Journey and were stronger for it. They alone had made the journey.

In my life, it has not been the good times, but rather the hard times, the struggle through the trauma, the disaster, and dealing with the negative aspects of it. How I handled it has brought me to a new place in life, with a new understanding of myself, strength, a proud sense of being, and resilience. I was my light that shone. I now understand more of what Hank and Hale Makua spoke of when they instructed us that we learn from the negative, the hard trials, as we learn to climb up our own Mountain.

Although working through the trauma can be filled with anguish, it can also bring many blessings when we face it. I found those blessings, and I came out a stronger being. With the brain damage, I learned I was not my brain, but I have a mental soul. I learned to work around memory loss. I learned to let go and find that the true me was still there.

To lose my arm/hand and neck movement for a while meant I couldn't even hold a paintbrush to create. I learned my physical soul was resilient and could be used in new ways. I was not my physical body either. I taught myself how to paint with my feet. I physically felt the joy.

I was something more, much more. Learning from this negative experience, feeling the anger, the rage, and the tears. Facing the realization of these hard experiences taught me how to let my own light shine forth and tether to it.

I often asked myself before, "Do I have a right to be powerful?

This thought hurt, knowing that I never thought that I was powerful in my own right, and that I deserved anything but crumbs thrown my way, but I did. I was powerful, and my voice was needed. It was my voice, and I had survived for a reason. The powers that be kept me alive for a reason.

I no longer need to search outside of myself for belonging; my boundaries are fortified. I did not need to fear death; I could live. In my struggle for total healing in mind, body, and spirit, I navigated a path of learning to create again. I learned to create what makes me happy and what I truly love. By losing almost everything I had known, I learned to let my own light shine, for myself, and that's what I could give.

About Heidi Zin

Art has been a guiding rhythm in my life since childhood. Drawn to color, shape, pattern, and texture, I use creative expression to explore the natural world, human emotion, and the interplay of light and shadow, influenced by water, shamanism, and a search for inner meaning.

I studied at Ringling School of Art and earned a BFA in sculpture and drawing from CCA, along with a certificate in Expressive Arts Healing. My early environmental work received the California Discovery Award from Henry Hopkins, and I spent decades teaching art and sharing the belief that creativity is foundational to our humanity.

After surviving a near-death accident in the Channel Islands that left me with a traumatic brain injury, my life and art transformed. Today I create as an Inner Medicine Woman Artist. Through my paintings, drawings, and my book *Falling In and Through*, I invite others to witness the beauty of transformation and the healing power within creative expression. HeidiZinArt.com

2

THE MIRROR IS NO LONGER SO SCARY
BY CLAUDIA MICCO

When the #METOO movement finally detonated, I felt something dangerously close to relief. Excitement, even. It was quickly followed by guilt when I took a hard look at my own silence.

I grew up on the older end of Generation X, when the rules were clear. Keep your mouth shut. Do not cause trouble. And for God's sake, do not be dramatic. Especially if you are a girl. Silence was not a personal failing. It was a life skill; it kept us out of trouble. We were raised to believe it built character. Or at least kept the adults comfortable. Same thing, apparently.

I buried my first sexual violation so deeply, around eight or nine years old, that by adulthood, I nearly convinced myself it had not happened.

Or that it did not count, that it did not matter, or that it was somehow my fault for not stopping it. But it was real. And it happened more than once by more than one person.

I have since learned how common this is. Women and men walking around with competent smiles, successful lives, and bodies holding memories we never quite unpack. Hands under shirts and down pants. The confusion of shame fused with fear so tightly that we forget we are holding our breath.

By twenty, I was married and living in Alameda, California, fully committed to outrunning the past. I was very good at survival. I found a man who understood my quirkiness, and I left my hometown when I was eighteen. My new husband was loving and kind, but the safer I felt, the louder the old ghosts became. It's as if the quiet safety we created gave them space to be the loudest voices in my head. Nothing wakes up old trauma like a safe relationship and decent health insurance.

One weekend, we stayed at a seaside inn in Jenner. Ocean views. Seals barking offshore. Candlelight. Long romantic walks. The brochure version of happiness.

The kind of place where happiness is implied, and disappointment is optional. I should have been enchanted. Instead, when he reached for me that first night, my body froze.

I had always believed I loved sex. Or at least, I loved getting through it. I dissociated, role played, disappeared just enough to make it work. I became very good at leaving without technically going anywhere. That night, though, the walls I had built were too solid. I couldn't escape myself or the reality that I was with someone real, a man I loved and actually wanted to connect with. I could not leave myself anymore.

The next evening at dinner, white tablecloths, wine, ocean air slipping through the windows, everything looked perfect. He reached across the table and asked gently what was going on with me.

My throat closed. Panic allowed only tears during dinner. I tried to explain, barely, that childhood memories were surfacing. I couldn't name them properly. He stopped me and said quietly that he knew that he had always thought something had happened to me.

Relief and terror collided. He saw me. I should have been grateful. Instead, I recoiled. We were so young. Untrained in healing. Two people trying to love without language. That distance became our ultimate undoing.

So, I ran. Again.

New city. New friends. Same internal furniture. And like a strange magnet, I found people carrying similar secrets. At a gym in Marin County, I met a tall, poised blonde woman, whom I was immediately drawn to. Over lunch one day, she casually mentioned her years of sexual abuse by a family member and said she attended a Survivors Anonymous healing group meeting.

I had never heard those words spoken out loud before. Survivors. Meeting. Daylight. As if trauma had office hours.

She invited me to sit in the circle. I went, heart pounding, and listened as strangers spoke plainly about things I had never let myself feel. I did not speak. I hovered on the edge. Without realizing it, I had found a mirror. It was full of cracks. This moment of connection was my first tiny step toward healing. Still, I clung to the old rules. Suck it up. Shut it down. Move on.

Then came what I thought was my big break. I became fitness director for three Bay Area gyms and was sent to a conference in Los Angeles with my boss and coworkers. We were supposed to share a room meant for four. I had not even questioned it at the time. Corporate budgeting decisions are rarely made with women's nervous systems in mind. One coworker missed her flight. Another disappeared with a stranger. I was left alone with him.

He was not a monster. He was just big. And drunk. And my boss.

When he moved toward the bed, my body reacted before my brain caught up. Panic surged. I wanted to run. Instead, I froze. I froze in a way I still cannot explain. He tried to kiss me. I mouthed no. My body shut down. I dissociated and let it happen. I felt I had no way out at the time.

Afterward, I scrubbed myself raw in the shower, crawled into the other bed, and pretended nothing had happened.

He saw only silence and compliance. Later, he bragged to other managers about that night. I was mortified.

I said nothing. Who would believe me? I stayed, worked in that quiet hell for a few more months, then received a raise, as if silence were a performance metric. Apparently, silence came with benefits. I quit that job at the first opportunity and tried to forget about it.

It took three years before I told a soul what happened.

When #METOO finally arrived, it gave me hope and grief. I admired those young women who spoke immediately, even as they were doubted, blamed, and dissected. I envied their courage. I wished I had their language, their permission, their refusal to swallow it whole. I could never imagine having such courage.

Instead, I carried guilt for surviving quietly. What was wrong with me?

But here is the irony. Even in my silence, I had been collecting tools that would keep my sanity. My first memory surfaced when I was eighteen in a Gestalt dance class on Maui. Our teacher, Joan, a psychologist, dancer, and radiant relic of the sixties, had us draw our bodies, meditate, move, and visualize. In one class, during a meditation focused on the pelvis, memories erupted without warning. I realized then that I had no control over what others had done to me. I could only work with my own journey from that point forward, which included keeping this all to myself. Probably not as smart an idea as I thought.

That realization did not make me immune to mistakes. Being young and female still made me overly trusting.

Still made me vulnerable. But it did give me some tools to practice. Meditation. Yoga. Tai Chi.

Ways to be inside my body without fleeing it. Touch, however, remained complicated. Sex was possible, but never whole. I dissociated. I pretended. I never felt entirely present.

Near my 32nd birthday, I made a decision that surprised even me. I would become a massage therapist.

Massage school in Hawaii was spiritual, private, and demanding. We touched and were touched every day for over a year. Slowly, something shifted. I learned the difference between appropriate touch and violation. Between intimacy and threat. Between being present and being trapped.

Touch without sex meant intimacy without danger.

I became very good at it very fast. My strong background in anatomy and physiology, coupled with my empathetic nature, helped. Perfectionism helped. I worked in hotels, private practice, and clinical settings.

I worked on thousands of bodies, from A-list celebrities and dignitaries to everyday people. At one point, even the Prince of Morocco ended up on my table. The body does not lie. It tells its story whether we are ready or not.

What surprised me most was that my work was never about fixing others. It was about becoming comfortable with myself. Touch no longer meant danger. It became information.

That did not mean the world stopped being the world. Massage therapists see their share of inappropriate behavior. By then, I knew the difference. I had boundaries. I had language. I had a spine. I have stories that would shock you, but still make you laugh out loud.

Massage therapy freed me from shame and guilt that never belonged to me in the first place. It gave me agency over my body. It taught me that trauma lives in tissue, but so does healing.

Trauma did not stop with sexual violations. I survived a critical car accident. A major earthquake. The AIDS epidemic. The Lahaina Fire. The deaths of my dearest f friends and parents. Loss layered on loss. Trauma, it turns out, is not a specialty item. It is a universal experience with different packaging. No one escapes with a clean record.

Trauma can flatten you. It can make you disappear into your bed for days. It can convince you that no one would understand. It will make you think you are unlovable. It will tell you that you are broken beyond repair.

Or eventually, it can sharpen you.

What mattered was not what happened to me. It was what I did afterward. Each time, I gathered something useful.

Each time, I carried it forward. Blaming God, society, parents, or perpetrators was easy.

Meaning took work.

I am still a work in progress. I remind myself often that shame keeps us stuck. Curiosity opens doors. Trauma does not define us, but it demands a response.

Mine is this. I stayed. I learned. I built a life that fits me now. I help others feel safe in their bodies. I laugh often.

Dark humor counts. Irony helps smooth out the edges. If you can still laugh, even sideways, you are already ahead of the game. The power it once had over me has somewhere to go now.

If there is hope here, it is not that trauma disappears. It does not. It becomes part of who we are and who we become. But it does not have to be the whole story. Over time, it can shift, soften, and even shape us in ways we never expected. We become more than the worst thing that ever happened to us.

And that feels like something worth holding on to.

The mirror is no longer so scary.

About Claudia Micco

Claudia Micco is a wellness educator and author living on Maui, Hawaii. With a background in fitness, massage therapy, and mind-body practices, she has spent four decades helping people feel stronger, safer, and more at home in their bodies. Her work now focuses on movement and wellness for older adults and people living with neurological conditions.

3

STAYING STRONG AND CARRYING ON
BY JILL ROTH

What the hell happened with my life?

How did I get here?

How did I allow someone in so deep that it broke me?

It was a warm August day when, upon returning from an out-of-state trip with my sister and our kids, I fell prey, yet again, to a meticulous trap laid out by my husband, the man I spent ten years in servitude, while he spent those years tearing me down, manipulating me to become the drone of his own liking. And it was this very trap that catapulted me into the next chapter of my life, but one that landed me, before that, into handcuffs in the back of a police car on my way to jail.

Life has a weird way of standing still in moments of trauma.

There was absolutely nothing for me to do or nowhere for me to go. I was trapped in the police car and in my life. So I paused, I prayed, I breathed, and I put myself in the present moment to remain grounded in my body, for that is all I had. It was all I could control. And I desperately needed to have control of something, anything.

I am alive,
I am breathing,
I am safe. For now.

Upon arriving at the jail, I was relieved to be free of the tight confines of the police car, but what awaited me was unclear. At least the car was quiet and predictable. But soon I would find the chaos resume as I was ushered to have my mug shots and fingerprints and then placed in an individual holding cell with a tiny toilet. I did the only thing I could do: lie on the bench and cry. The metal from the bench pierced through me like ice to skin, but I did not move. I did not care. I was numb.

Numb to it all and nothing mattered anymore, especially my comfort. I did not deserve to be comfortable.

I am not worthy of a good life.
I am not a good person.
I get what I deserve.

In jail, they do not give you a grand tour; they do not explain what they are doing with you step-by-step, and they are not required to answer your questions. You are not worthy of the breath to do so, and it was a reflection of exactly how I felt about myself.

I am not worthy of the air I breathe.

Thinking I would be in that holding cell all night, I was slightly relieved when the door was opened, and I was ushered to another small room down the hall. Upon entering the small room, however, my relief vanished. Before me, at the end of the room, a window with a six-inch gap at the bottom, and to the left, a shower- no curtain. A portly woman in uniform stood in the window. Behind her was what looked like a metal clothing rack from the dry cleaner, personal items swaying in bags hanging above her.

"Please remove your clothes and bring them to me. You can keep your undergarments." Then she looked at me again. "Except the panties. Shower with the soap provided, then come back for your clothes."

"Why can't I keep panties?" I asked. "You can't wear them, they're pink."

I looked at her, dumbfounded.

"Well, if I knew I was going to get arrested today, I would have worn white panties." I retorted, instantly regretting it. *Just shut up, Jill. Keep your head down and say "yes, ma'am," and "No, ma'am."*

But the panties were not my biggest problem. I looked over at the shower, again with no privacy, and stood there for a minute, my mouth agape.

I never undressed in front of my own mother, let alone a stranger!

However, the look on the female officer's face through the window made it clear that I had limited options. I humbly walked to the window, stripped myself of my only possessions, including my dignity, and shoved my clothes through the opening in the plexiglass. I walked over to the shower and submerged myself in the running water, scrubbing my hair with the shampoo as if I were trying to scrub away the last twenty-four hours and the damning words swirling around in my head.

Abandonment.
Betrayal.
Deception.
Control.

I gave all my sovereignty away when I surrendered to the manipulation and control of others, especially my husband.

Because standing my ground and making my own decisions always ended up pushing me up against a proverbial brick wall. So I surrendered. And with it, the control over my own fate. And jail was no different.

I wanted to stay in the warmth of the shower with my eyes closed indefinitely, but remembered I was not alone. I finished quickly and toweled off.

"Here." The officer shoved a folded-up orange garment and matching slides.

Once dressed, I was ushered down the hall, full commando, in my iconic 'Orange Is the New Black' jumpsuit. We arrived a few minutes later at a grey metal door, similar to the ten others we had just passed.

Using her badge to gain access, the female officer opened the door to reveal a large room divided down the middle by a half-cement wall. Round tables with attached seats bolted to the ground were to the left, and two long rows of metal bunk beds were to the right. To my direct left was an opening in the wall that housed a bathroom: two sinks, exposed toilets and showers, again with no privacy. To the right, another female police officer sat at a metal desk reminiscent of the teachers in the Catholic school I attended many years ago.

The officer who brought me into the room led me over to the end bunk, and the heads of the other female inmates swiveled in my direction, their gaze fixed on the newbie in curiosity. I was shown a small trunk next to the bed that held white sheets, towels, and some sparse toiletries. There was even a personal roll of toilet paper.

I glanced at the bed I would inhabit for the night: one-inch grey plastic pad, no pillow. I peered down again into the open trunk, thinking maybe I just did not see it. Nope.

What was I expecting? The Four Seasons?

Before she left, the female officer turned to face me. "Are you hungry?"

"Actually, yes." I managed. She nodded and turned to leave. Twenty minutes later, she returned with a bologna sandwich, a half-inch thick, not something I usually would have normally eaten on 'the outside,' but I gobbled it up with gratitude.

Soon enough, some of the other girls started flocking around me. Girls with names like 'Florida' and 'Montana' obviously signifying their home state.

"What are you in for?" They would ask.
"I hit my husband," I said sheepishly.
"Ah, just like Maria over there," Florida said in commiseration, turning around and pointing at a middle-aged Hispanic woman. "I'm sure you had a good reason." She said with a wink.

After a few conversations, I got the sense that the other inmates thought I wasn't meant to be there. Like I didn't belong. But I did belong. I broke the law. Despite what I went through in the years leading up to this point, it did not change the fact that I did something illegal, and I was called out on it. I was no different than Florida or Montana.

There was an unspoken solidarity among the women. Some talked to each other, others kept to themselves, but no one harassed me or treated me poorly. It was ironically peaceful, unlike my life on the outside. Lights out even brought games reminiscent of summer camp, as the girls laughed and tossed their toilet paper across the room from bunk to bunk, white streamers of paper flying through the air. I closed my eyes and imagined myself in another time, in another place.

With the edge of my mattress rolled up to fashion a pillow, I willed myself to sleep. But it wasn't just the camaraderie of my fellow inmates keeping me awake; it was the dread that pounded in my head.

The dread of what was to come. The dread that I may have just lost custody of my son. And the only thing that could save me was one small plastic object: the SIM card from my camera.

But where was it?
Did I pick it up?
Did I give it to my sister?
Did my sister pick it up?
Or worse...Did my ex get it?

The SIM card, which housed the camera's memories, was ejected from the camera when my husband ripped it from my hands and smashed it to the ground while I was in the midst of taking a video of him removing unwarranted possessions from our joint home during our divorce. His action in that moment triggered in me a storm of repressed frustration, anger, resentment, and self-vindication, whipping powerfully and forcefully in the form of fists beating into my husband's muscular two-hundred-forty-pound frame.

And I knew that video of him taking the camera away from me on that SIM card could be my only saving grace from the mess I found myself in.

My mind was reeling, my stomach in knots. I had to get through the night, so I could talk to my sister.

Sleep, dammit, sleep!!

The morning came early and abruptly, accompanied by blinding fluorescent lights that served as a vicious alarm clock. But it also came with a schedule.

Thank goodness. Schedules I can do.

First was breakfast, which consisted of powdered eggs with some seasoned mystery meat, oatmeal, and orange juice. Next, tasks were posted on a paper on the wall. My task was to use a spray bottle of cleaner to wipe off all the bunk beds. I worked quickly but efficiently, eyeing the phones on the wall across the room, knowing I could use them as soon as I finished.

I was limited to one call, so I called my sister. I drilled her on the SIM card, which she thankfully had in her possession. I breathed a sigh of relief. She also filled me in on the progress she made with securing a lawyer.

Before hanging up, my sister said with a shaky voice, "I'm sorry, Jill, I'm so sorry!"

"Hey, it's not your fault. I got myself into this mess. I am so glad you were here to help me with all of this! Who else would I have had?"

I hung up and shed a tear of relief. It might just be okay. But the day was not over, and I was at the mercy of my new dictators. In a short time, we were lined up to be patted down before leaving the dormitory. Chained together at the wrists, we marched in a line like preschool kids on a field trip, where they deposed us in an outdoor area- a small rectangular space, cement block walls 20 feet up, barbed wire encasing the top. It was surreal, like a movie, a horror movie.

I kept my head down and walked the ten-by-twenty-foot space, briskly, with purpose, as if I had one. The only thing I could depend on in that moment was the earth beneath my feet and the fresh air I breathed into my lungs.

If I tried hard enough, I could almost imagine I was somewhere else-a park, a trail, anywhere else. I would look up to the sky, however, and see the metal spikes encircling the area, reminding me that freedom was a precious commodity. A perspective I knew I would carry with me for the rest of my life.

Upon re-entering the facility, the officers split the group and took some of us to a small room with a TV at one end, a table, and a single chair. On the other end, ten chairs lined the wall in a half circle. There were men already in the room, which, for some reason, surprised me. One by one, the judge called us up to the table to discuss the details of our arrest, the bail, and the judgment.

Then it dawned on me.
This is a makeshift court.

Then I heard my name. I stood and walked over to the table, pulling out a chair.

I took a deep breath, my palms sweating as I sat facing the tiny, yet ironically intimidating man on the screen. The stern-looking judge, eyes narrowed, informed me of the charges I was facing. I tried to rebut, but he was not open to feedback and scolded me for doing so, taking the opportunity to impress upon me the severity of my crimes.

In the background, behind the judge, sat my sister next to a well-dressed young man whom I did not recognize. The younger gentleman stood up to address the judge and introduced himself as a lawyer from the same law firm as my divorce attorney. He pleaded with the judge to grant me a reprieve from my situation, pending my attendance at trial at a later date. The judge agreed and turned back to me for more reprimand. I clenched my fists tight, fighting back the sting of tears. My ego was on fire!

But I am a nice girl! I shouted in my head. I was the good Catholic schoolgirl who did everything she was told. She followed the rules, she got straight A's, and she had awards and trophies that proved exemplary behavior.

She was the girl who put herself out to make everyone else comfortable, who gave of herself, over and over...And MY character was in question?

What about my ex! WHAT ABOUT MY EX!!

I no longer knew who I was. I fit into everyone else's boxes so neatly for so many years that I forgot I even had my own box. I felt so betrayed by the person I married, and now I was betrayed by the person I thought I was.

Who am I?
What am I supposed to do now?

My future, my life, and the custody of my one-year-old were all in question.

Thanks to my sister's efforts in securing a lawyer for me, I was released that day.

Only one night in jail, one night on that hard, cold bed, only one humiliating shower in front of strangers.

But what I failed to recognize was that my humiliation came long before the handcuffs on my wrists in front of my neighbors, or the mug shots and fingerprints, or even the belittling court case. It came when I allowed my husband to treat me as though I were his property. And then it dawned on me. I had been imprisoned a lot longer than one night, and it was going to take many more nights to set myself completely free. Free of the mindset that kept me trapped. The mindset that I was his, and his alone. That no one could ever love me like he did.

That I did not need my family. He was all I needed. That I had to wear what he said, and do as he said, and become exactly who he wanted me to be, to fit, to belong, because I craved so desperately to be something to somebody, therefore surrendering my own sovereignty in the process.

Many years prior, I stood at the church altar where my husband and I were married, a God-like voice booming in my head, *"You will not be married to him for the rest of your life."* A sign I ignored, but one that left an indelible mark as a sick warning sign of what was to come. And after years of proof, in the form of abuse, I finally decided to leave the marriage. *Oh, no. Not for myself.* But for the son that took us years to have. I was not willing to risk continuing the cycle of abuse, demonstrating to my son how a husband treats a wife.

Saving myself was not a big enough reason to leave, but my son was. And in me saving him, he saved me. And I now knew I was something to somebody. Maybe not to myself yet. That would take years to discover. But I was somebody to my son. I was his mother. And after the title of wife no longer served me, I took the only other title I could have at that point in my life: mother. And that title became the very reason I did everything in my power from that point on to stay strong and carry on. And so I did.

About Jill Roth

As a life philosophy, Jill Roth promotes empowered, well-rounded healing by fostering a healthy connection among mind, body, and spirit through her writing, singing/songwriting, and fitness expertise. She deeply believes in the power of shared experiences and uses her own journey to support and encourage others on theirs.

Jill lives in central Ohio with her two youngest sons and inspires them to live their best lives, despite any circumstances they may encounter along the way. She welcomes you to connect and indulge in her other written works and inspirational videos on Substack via https://substack.com/@yourbodyawarenesscoach

4

THE STEAL
A STORY OF BETRAYAL, BLOODLINE, AND BECOMING
BY HABAKA KFJ

"When grief and betrayal silenced me, my heritage called me back, and from that dark season I didn't just return to music, I returned to my roots, founding my own record label and creating work no one could ever take from me again."

The Steal

That summer, my life sounded like a possibility. I moved between recording sessions and live performances, pouring long days, early mornings, and warm nights into songs I believed were opening a new chapter. After a successful launch of a Single and a Christmas CD, we had formed an LLC together, a shared name made from our initials, a symbol of trust and forward motion. I was totally convinced this is it, I've finally got the right people who really believe in me, who truly are vested in me for all of the right reasons. Did you know that people can put on a façade to get what they want from you for years, which will make you think that it's nearly impossible for anything to go wrong and that it can only get better. The EP was recorded, nearly finished, waiting only for final mastering once I returned from a short trip to the United States. It was supposed to be a vacation; a pause before the music moved fully into the world. I packed my suitcase, thinking I was stepping away briefly, never imagining I was walking out of one life and into another.

"I Knew I Wasn't Going Back"

The shift didn't happen with an announcement. No grand moment. No speech. It came in the quiet rhythm of caregiving, medication times, doctor visits, and watching my father's strength move in reverse. Each day, I told myself this was temporary. I would go back. The studio was waiting.

The mixes would be finished, and it was sounding amazing. My summer of work would continue forward. But as the days stretched,

I began to measure time differently; not in sessions or shows, but in breaths, in good hours and hard nights.

I remember looking at my suitcase still partly packed, sitting in the corner like a promise I had made to another version of myself. And I knew. Not from logic, but from a place deeper than ambition. My father needed me in a way that had no substitute, no postponement, no delegation. Music could wait. (It's only my lifelong music career) That's how I brainwashed myself to think about it, because deep down inside, I didn't want to give it up. Life could not. (Why is this happening?)

The decision didn't feel heroic. It felt heavy. It felt like setting something precious down without knowing if I would ever be able to pick it back up again. I didn't know then what this choice would cost. I only knew that love had made the decision before I had the words to say it.

Betrayal - "The Steal"

While my days were measured by my father's needs, decisions about my music were being made elsewhere.

An official video bearing the title of the EP and the EP we had created in trust after a full summer of work, was still waiting to be mastered, or so I believed. The agreement had been simple: I would return from vacation and contribute my share, and we would complete it together. But caregiving doesn't run on a schedule, and my return date kept getting pushed further back.

They Knew Why

They knew I wasn't absent because of disinterest or neglect. I was sitting beside a hospital bed, learning how to live inside anticipatory grief. Still, without me and without my participation in the final step, he chose to move forward. He paid for the master himself and finalized the EP cover. And in doing so, the ground beneath our agreement shifted. What had been shared was no longer shared. It was a company takeover from both of them.

The music was released. Ownership changed hands in practice, if not in spirit. And I was told I could not promote the very work my voice and face carried.

There are moments when loss comes from life. And there are moments when loss comes from people.

This was both at once. While I was preparing to say goodbye to my father, I was also saying goodbye to a piece of my own voice; not because I chose to, but because I was not in a position to fight.

That was the steal.

Aftermath "The Silence"

When my father passed, the world did not crash the way I expected. It went quiet. A stillness settled over everything, as if sound itself had stepped back out of respect. I moved through the days numb, carrying paperwork, memories, and a tiredness that sleep could not fix.

The music situation lingered in the background like an echo I didn't want to hear. I had no fight left in me, not for business, not for explanations, not even for songs.

For the first time in my life, singing felt far away from me. Not gone, just unreachable, like a room in a house I could no longer enter. Music had always been where I went to feel alive, but now it reminded me of loss, of what had been taken, of what had ended, of who was no longer here to hear me sing. I didn't announce that I was done. I just stopped reaching for it.

Grief had taken my father. Betrayal had taken the project. And somewhere in between, I felt like I had lost my voice, too.

"The Remembering"

I didn't watch the film because I felt inspired. I watched it because I felt empty. The house was quiet in a way that only comes after loss, and I needed something to fill the space, even if only for a couple of hours. When the story of Bessie Smith began to unfold (portrayed by Queen Latiffa),

I wasn't thinking about music industry politics or unfinished projects. I was simply watching a life shaped by struggle, survival, and song.

But somewhere in the middle of the film, something shifted. Her story didn't feel distant. It felt familiar, not in the details, but in spirit. The resilience, the lineage of sound born from pain and endurance. The way music wasn't a career choice, but a lifeline passed down.

And I realized I wasn't just watching history. I was looking at my roots.

For the first time since everything had fallen apart, the music did not feel like a place of betrayal. It felt like home.

What had been taken from me belonged to a system. What was calling me back belonged to something older than all of it. Older than contracts, Older than ownership, Older than loss.

In that quiet recognition, the silence inside me softened. Not because the pain was gone, but because I understood something I hadn't before: my voice did not begin with that project, and it did not end with it either.

It was a heritage.

This moment is the spiritual pivot.

Not "I'll show them."

But "I remember who I am."

I thought the silence meant something had ended. After my father passed, after the music was taken, after I closed the LLC and shut the door on everything we had built, I believed my voice had left with that season. Singing felt like reopening a wound. But in my emptiness, I watched the story of Bessie Smith, and something deeper than industry, contracts, or betrayal stirred in me. I saw my lineage. I saw that this music was never just business; it was inheritance, survival, and soul passed down through blood and history. What had been stolen was a recording. What remained was a calling.

From that dark place, Husky Tone Records was born, and Heritage Blue rose not from opportunity, but from remembrance.

They could claim a master, but they could not claim my roots. And in returning to them, I found my voice again, not as something the world gave me, but as something no one could ever take away.

"Rebirth-What Couldn't Be Stolen"

That night did not bring a sudden burst of energy or certainty. Grief does not move that way. But something steadier took its place, a quiet knowing. If music were truly my inheritance, then it could not be given to me by partners, and it could not be taken away by them either.

It had lived in me long before contracts and would remain long after them.

Out of that realization, Husky Tone Records was born, not as a business decision first, but as a declaration.

A reclaiming of ground. A place where my voice, my story, and my roots could exist without permission.

And from that same soil came Heritage Blue, a work shaped not by opportunity, but by remembrance. It carried my father, my mother, my grandmother, my grandfather, my lineage, my sorrow, my strength, everything that season had carved into me.

I once thought The Steal was the story of something being taken. But now I understand it was also the story of something being returned. They could claim a master recording. But they could not claim my origin. They could not claim my calling. And they could not claim the voice that rose again, deeper and more rooted than before.

What I lost was real. But what I found was mine, and what a gift to receive. Hugs

About Habaka KFJ

Habaka KFJ is an Award-Winning international Blues, Jazz, and Gospel vocalist whose life and music are deeply intertwined with heritage, healing, and resilience. Known for a voice that carries both strength and vulnerability, her journey has been shaped as much by life's quiet battles as by the stage. A caregiver, storyteller, and independent artist, she founded Husky Tone Records as an act of reclamation, creating space for music born from lineage rather than industry definition. Her work honors the belief that even in seasons of loss, the roots that formed us remain unshaken. Through song and story, she explores how grief, love, and identity shape the voices we carry forward.

5

TUESDAY EVENING IN THE UNIVERSE BY GABRIEL LOVEMORE

I am eleven. It is a Tuesday evening. My parents and my younger brother are sitting at the table for dinner. I am silent. I have been silent for two weeks now. I don't look up. I don't interact more than the compulsory minimum. I look down at my plate. Every cell in me is waiting for dinner to be over. My body is in the kitchen. My spirit is hiding in my bedroom.

Two weeks prior. I am sitting at my desk writing, just like every time I do homework. My room is small. Our flat is small.

We live in a high-rise building. A world of concrete. The delirious vision of some architect's idea of a modern city. Limited car traffic. Boxes piled up sky high. We call them "rabbit cages" in French. Plenty of places to walk. As many places to be isolated. Bullied. Beaten up.

Earlier that year, Mum bought us tickets for the Charlie Chaplin retrospective at the cultural center. My brother and I would not miss a session. I remember walking out one afternoon, still vibrating from the film. A couple of larger kids pulled me aside and beat me up. For no reason other than that it was possible. Adults kept walking by. No one stopped. No one stopped them. Hospital. X-rays. By now, I know the routine. It was not the first time. I knew it would not be the last.

My Mum calls for dinner. My dad walks in, and I quickly hide the envelope I am writing. After dinner, he asks: What is this letter about? I am silent. I don't want to share. They ask again. I resist. Refuse. I don't want to talk about it. My refusal yields no results. My parents walk in. Open the drawer. And the envelope.

I am furious. Enraged. And so small. Powerless. "This is mine," my thoughts are screaming. "Mine." I drown in rage. My body feels like a stone. Dense.

Contracted. I push my hands in my pockets to hide my fists. I want to explode. I can't.

My mum reads the letter. My dad watches over her shoulder. Their faces shift. Concern to smile. Then laughter.

Relief, probably. Their son is not on drugs. Just in love. But I am eleven. And my secret garden is now a joke at the kitchen table. That is unforgivable.

For months, I have dreamt of a girl in my class. She is thin with long hair. I can't even speak to her without blushing. So, I avoid her. Despite wanting just the opposite. Her name has slipped my memory long ago. But the first feeling of love is still here.

I have written several letters by then. Some I wrote in my own blood. Enough letters to know I will never find the courage to send them. The letters are an outlet. A dream. My secret garden. A little treasure chest behind my ribs. The place where, at eleven, I started to water the seed of love.

In this concrete jungle at the edge of the city, every parent is paranoid about drugs. I have no clue what drugs are. Never seen any. Never taken any. My entire life is about survival. Trying to be safe. Outside, my eyes constantly scan the environment. I avoid corners. Isolated places. I hold on to my school bag, wishing it were a James Bond device. Some miraculous tool to escape impossible situations.

A few years earlier, an undiagnosed condition stunted my growth for two years. My younger brother is now taller than me. So is everyone else in my class. You would think that being smaller makes you less visible. Not in my experience. I became a bully magnet. I started to fear the end of class. The walk back home. Every group of children was a potential enemy. In an instant, I could become someone's strategy to show others how strong they were. By proving to everyone how weak I was.

I learned that to belong, you had to submit. To suffer. To be ridiculed. The alternative was loneliness.

My life was not extraordinary or special. My parents fed me. Loved me. Took care of my education.

They did not beat me. They did not starve me or tie me to a pipe in the basement. I was not born in a refugee camp. I did not experience famine.

And yet, I learned in a very subtle way that I was not safe. And that if I could not trust my parents, then I could not trust anyone. My whole life was designed with that blueprint in mind.

This became a permanent companion. An initial bite that, like a chisel to a sculptor, created the architecture that would inform every choice after.

From it, I derived great strength. I became self-sufficient. Resourceful. I learned to adapt to almost any dysfunctional situation. Being smaller gave me an infinite appetite for growth. For learning. A hunger to evolve.

It also sent me on the road of service. When my muscles and bones finally caught up, I dedicated them to helping others in my situation. Some invisible brotherhood of the unseen, the bullied, those too small to make choices for themselves.

I also learned to be a lone wolf. To be alone. Isolated. Always on guard. I built an image of strength and confidence. I don't blush anymore. I don't cry either, unless I really let myself. It has cost me a lot in relationships. I kept choosing people who could not harm me. Until they did anyway.

Mostly, it has brought immense sadness and loneliness. After two weeks, the rage started to dissolve. I spoke again. But the promise I made to myself never changed. I would never share anything important with my parents. Ever. And I never did.

Two years after these events, my parents moved to another place. A large house. A smaller town. Closer to nature. No drugs or no violence.

That is what they said. For me, it did not change. But I had lost my friends in the move. Lost my alliances. The people that I knew were safe. And I had to rebuild that.

Moving was just another challenge to overcome. Certainly, did not feel safe either.

I forgave. I moved on. As an adult, I visited them once in a while, coming back from a mission far away.

I did what good children do. But the door to my private life was forever closed to them.

I am in my mid-sixties now. I still scan rooms when I walk in. My eyes find the exits. I never sit with my back to a door or a window. Old habits. I am a guide. A coach. A teacher. All subtle ways to keep the space with others. Other recipes to be safe.

Somewhere along the way, the boy at that table became the man who chose the dangerous places. The battlefields. The cliffs. The depths. Not running from fear.

Walking toward it. Again and again. Until it became familiar. Until it became a kind of home.

The constant living in fear became one of my greatest assets. I was able to function everywhere dysfunctional.

In war zones. With guns everywhere. Hyperawareness became a management skill that paid well.

September 1991. I am walking down a street in Kinshasa, Zaire. The country is a giant mess. Two men jump out of a car and try to grab me by the arms. In a fraction of a second, I see their intention.

Before they know it, my reflexes have kicked in and I am out of reach. In that second, my eleven-year-old self saved me. Faster than the adult I had become could have. Hyperawareness is a curse with a silver lining. I can keep hundreds of conversations going without losing one. I walk on the pavement like you drive a car. Aware of who is left, right, behind. Who is fast and who cannot hold the line? Constantly evaluating the possibility of conflict.

For this, I have lived a life in constant fight or flight. My hobbies were adrenaline addictions. My skills to display excellence in dysfunction. And my sleep, something only possible in dreams.

My parents were not villains. They were afraid. They saw the concrete jungle and its dangers and tried to protect their son. They could not see that the danger I needed protection from was elsewhere. Closer. Already inside the flat.

I don't carry this story as a wound anymore. I carry it the way a tree carries the scar where a branch broke off. It changed its shape. Directed the growth. Made me reach a different direction for light.

Sometimes, jokingly, when people ask me how I came to LA, I respond, "Running away from my Mum." Barely a joke.

Often, I wonder, "Is it possible to truly feel safe?" "Was life even made to be safe in the first place?" I don't know. I have learned to speak at the dinner table. I have learned to share about my private life. To be vulnerable. Authentic. I have extensive training in martial arts that I never had to use. Not even in the worst places. Everything tells me I am safe now.

Yet I still host that place within. A 11-year-old boy who did not feel safe. He has been my lifelong companion.

About Gabriel Lovemore

Gabriel Lovemore holds a postgraduate degree in Political Science from La Sorbonne and spent 30 years working in conflict zones and refugee camps worldwide, learning to navigate impossible situations and help others do the same. That work became the foundation for everything that followed.

He is the author of *Locked In*, a novella exploring consciousness and reality through eight characters facing a day of crisis. He also writes regularly on Substack about coherence in a world of chaos, civilizational transition, and staying present as the ground shifts beneath our feet.

Gabriel now lives in Los Angeles, where he works with clients navigating major life transitions. His authority comes from seeing both the suffering created by Western policies and the systems behind them. His work as a coach, teacher, and writer, he says, is the same medicine delivered in different ways.

Find his writing at www.gabriellovemore.com

GRIEF IN PIECES
BY ELIZABETH CONVERSE

"What a Day"

And then there was my man. Last day to remember him by was the only day I knew he was sick. Ever. Well, maybe once.

You wonder how you deserved such an act of grace from an unknown God to deliver this man in my life. His famous last words — Elizabeth, I am your rock.

Your morning bike ride, working in the yard, laughing with the neighbor. You went shopping, brought home armloads of groceries and gallons of juice, trimmed the hedges, made dinner, and friends came over; we played cards and laughed for three hours. You never stopped laughing or carrying on, did you?

Finally, the evening of people and friends, rides, and talks ended. Did you win at cards that night? We watched TV and snuck in an old episode from Yellowstone. We went to bed, finally, tired. We kissed; I held your hot body tight.

You kept me close, tighter, your embrace, my refuge, and then I had to move away; you were so hot. My heater, I always called you.

We had perfect weather in the morning. Ranging from cool to warm with mottled cloud coverage, ideal for a morning ride into the North Fork, or the Santa Fe Dam, or maybe Flintridge-LaCanada and the Rose Bowl. Those well-worn bike trails, your roads to clarity, your personal setting for facing every experience or concern at work, home, garden, and barn. Your long meditative hours of silence, feeling breathing, your legs pumping, your laughing, gazing, witnessing — you, a beacon of warmth and light, restored yourself every day.

I ask you now, where are you?

I wanted to stop you from leaving. I tried to hold on to you. I held you, breathed into you. Pressed my hands fast against your chest, breathed into you. You were just having a bad moment. I brought the sirens for you. Held you, cried with you.

Your eyes were open, looking at me in surprise at the moment you left forever. As the golden glow of our love transmuted the misery of your going to glory and a perfect love we knew at its root. I sat there with you as you stared, as if in a shock of revelation, and together, our spirits held one another in timelessness, rocking in the endless sweetness and grace of our love.

Our love held us there, the goodness of all those years we pressed together in pages of countless experiences, experiments, misunderstandings, undertakings, challenges, all of it boiled down to one simple truth: Love is love is love.

———

"Then"

I am everything I see, touch, feel, and am. I am my heart opening in love, pain, sorrow, and tears — In glory, I am a world unfolding in my heart, in theirs, in mine. And we are all that we are. Together. So gentle. Alone together, we became a community. The gentle embrace of our days, times, loves, lives, and nature. The earth unfolding around us teaching us. Lessons of eternity. Of death. Of betrayal. Of time. Of Rebirth —

And now they are grown on their own. All Grown — and away, so far away — from me. We will return again. We will return again.

————

"Goodbyes"

Whisper again in my mind in the air do we need to say goodbye in the animal kingdom? It is definitive that greetings occur but uncertain if goodbyes do. Did you say goodbye or how else did the door slam shut — so love — how quickly did you die without a farewell. I was not available for your birth – on another planet, so to speak, and I can barely remember the hello, so no, goodbye, and

Whispers are not essential in every single hello, even though the sound of goodbye has a nice finality to it – you left me hanging at hello, don't try to make this about you or the screeching laughter of your last guffaw. I awaken in the night in the howls and the hoots when I hear the tumble of boulders and I am falling well at least I have said goodbye, once and for all as the night wails, the owls scream and the lion tamer is eaten alive.

In the photograph, she is walking away.

She is wearing blue jeans and a polo shirt

I don't know if she will come back or when

If ever who she'll be when she returns

And I remember when I said, I think she's back.

I think after years she is in there again.

I missed, oh how I missed this girl

The eternal mornings when she was gone

When she was so far away, I did not know if she would

ever come back at all or how she would be able to find her

way back.

Would I have been able to do what she had to,

but I did what I had to do.

Is that tensile strength?

You can't even write it down

Only Excerpts

And it's not a pissing contest, so you don't say a word, you

just wait…wait, holding your breath.

———

"But Now"

Who is this 40-year-old sitting in my living room? I nudge her, but can't feel anything. There are no edges, yet everything is sharp. I walk through the house, circling, wondering how long I can wait to unveil her. I don't stand passively, looking across the landscape of my life without reaction. I do not close in upon myself like a mollusk waiting for a storm to turn me over. I have urges and longings, desire and impatience. I seek meaning in the whiff of trees, the smashing of leaves between my fingers, and the reek of life.

But she stands timeless, her body perfected by discipline and subversion to prayer, wrapped in smoothness and silken diffusion. Only hair left on the counter reminds me she is still alive. This vessel in my living room who waits an eternal sentence, this mystery of life.

Sometimes, I pace these familiar floors, too. I try to engage in conversation, offer spoken words to create communion, and offer a shared sacred object to bridge the gap of silence, but she remains lodged irretrievably in a history I do not share.

I thought I could reach her. I thought I could help her. I thought. I thought. I thought she was too young for rust, too angry for defeat, too lost to come back.

How long? How long? I am getting death notices now. My body is a decaying temple. I am someone whose time is running out, and the gift of her presence remains elusive. What does she get from waiting me out? What are her stakes, except her mystery, or is it confusion?

I have seen her stand like a beacon of light, raise her hand, and watch people become silent. I have seen her golden in the light, a ray of hope.

I know of hope. What is her gain? What does she gain in losing me, in killing me, in abandoning me? Will she remember to go on, or will she remember nothing?
I walk circles in this house where we live apart—parallels rising, one grasping for length, the other seeing time, playing time, reeling time out like an elastic loop.
I wait. I can wait for her to emerge and live again.

———

"January 7, Breathing in the Wild"

In the morning, a month later, I woke with a sense of calm, although sadness lingered. Feelings of change settled in my chest with heaviness as I took my coffee outside to let a hazy sun light my face as a breeze rustled the leaves around me. After moments of breathing, I felt stillness within myself—a certainty that no matter what happened next, I was ready to meet it.

When I walked up the ridge, the wind was gusting up, vibrating the air into whorls and patterns, and the leaves were quivering and dancing. I heard birds chittering to one another as if in a warning. There were thousands of voices of insects warring in my ears — loudly, calling out to me; they never stopped. Then I thought I heard some of them go silent between gusts of air. I felt a rush of uncertainty with the winds and the insects' soundings. The sky was grey with smoke from the Palisades fire, and the nervous winds bounced against the parched landscape.

The dry grasses were sharp and perfumed with anisette and sage, bristling as they dried.

The canyon vegetation crackled underfoot. I pulled my hands through them and stuffed my pockets full, inhaling their odors, raising them to my face to smell their essence so closely I could almost taste them. This breathing was me again. My self smelling the wildness. Not the smokiness; that wasn't me. Tendrils of meaning drifted in and out of my thoughts.

I was grasping for insight. There were evocations of coherence, of seeing my life through to the next stop on the road. But I was wondering how much longer I could hold it together.

I stopped and breathed into the grasses once more. I felt the breath of love, the grace of the air, the leaves, the trees. Was I running out of love? I wouldn't wander; there was a destination now. There was money, and I would be safe. I had somewhere to go. It would be OK. I looked across the landscape at the rocks and shrubs that were my home. Would I need to leave this all behind and start a new chapter, one that would hold my children, my life, and the memories of him in a different place?

A knot formed in my stomach as I scanned the horizon, past the wind torrents and bending grasses. One spark, one misstep, could bring the fires here again. And I would be alone. These same beloved hills could be transformed overnight. I touched the amulet around my neck, feeling its weight, and breathed in, deeper, longer; I sat down on the ground to gather myself.

My spirit was as resilient as the land around me, and in that moment, I felt gratitude for the journey I had traveled. As the wind shifted again and again, I caught a trace of that metallic smokiness in the air, distant but unmistakable—a premonition that sent me hurrying back down the path, suddenly eager to check the news.

Do you remember? Did you like the first day of your life or the last better? Were you your own witness? What did it feel like to taste life in your mother's arms or die in my embrace? And now, do you remember what went on in between? Is your life made of memories, or is your life new again, wiped clean — have you been reborn?

I feel you through others, in each moment and movement, but the taste is full of you and breath of you and strength you have torn from me, when you left me utterly alone, before the new birth, before the fires, before the landslides, before the losses and devastation and illnesses tried to make another final toll.

I feel you breathing beside me. I still feel you touching me and holding me. You are my song, my poetry, you, my one, my only one.

————

"I'm Writing Now"

I'm writing now, sitting here — No, the food could be ready; I should reformat that page. What was the prompt? Oh — the mind games again. Where — I am — Sitting practicing that tapping exercise right side — left side breathe in 4 counts out 4 counts fire man's breath — Is that the mail man? I mean, mail person? Why is the wind howling now — it was a full year ago, oh well — it's my mind just wailing. Get the cup of tea, Elizabeth. Sit down, Elizabeth. You were telling me a story.

It was a really beautiful story, and I want to hear it. About the lonely girl whose mind ran away one day and never came back. Never came back, until it did when she finally arrived home with a smile on her face. When it did — like just now. Of all the stories I told myself when none of it made sense. When I could not even cry wolf —

About Elizabeth Converse

Elizabeth began writing as a restless child when her mother filled her bedroom with books to keep her from running away. She devoured stories and discovered the literary voice as a place to live inside her own life. Her father, a geologist and engineer, took his children into the hills and canyons, teaching them to read the land with a careful eye.

She has been writing ever since, and painting nearly as long, beginning in her twenties in New York while exploring theater and film. Writing reveals truths she sometimes only understands after they appear on the page, while painting allows her body to absorb what the words uncover.

Elizabeth has written plays, film scripts, journalism, poetry, and novels. She lives in Sierra Madre, California.

Grief in Pieces is her first work of autofiction, blending memoir and fiction to shape lived experience into narrative as she processed a series of traumatic events over two years.

7

THE YELLOW JACKET
BY JENNIFER PEDROTTI

My head snaps against the window. Once. Twice. Three times. The glass is cold and hard, and I think it might crack—either the window or my skull, I am not sure which will go first. I'm trying to remember where the police station is. Downtown somewhere. But the streets blur, and he's hitting me, and I can't think, and he's screaming you're getting lost," and maybe I was, perhaps I'd been lost for years.

It seemed like an hour had passed since he dragged me from the driver's seat, out the passenger's side of the car, into the house.

The shotgun barrel is cold against my cheek. I can see the perfect circle of metal within inches of my face. My head throbs in rhythm with my pulse—*thud-thud, thud-thud*—so loud it drowns out his screaming. I watch his finger on the trigger. Not moving, just resting there. The weight of a single finger between breathing and not breathing.

I knew the gun was loaded; he always kept it loaded. I could see the headlines in my mind's eye about my death.

Then God's voice was loud in my ear: **DON'T MOVE.**

So, I don't. I became stone while my husband—the man I loved at fourteen, married at twenty—decides whether I get to see twenty-one.

The neighbors never came. All that screaming—My screaming, glass shattering, my body hitting walls—and no one called. No one came. The duplex walls might as well have been soundproofed. Or maybe everyone just knew to mind their business when a man is teaching his wife a lesson.

The bathroom was supposed to be my happy place. Bright yellow. Cheerful. The shower curtain I picked out for our new home, torn down as he dragged me from the tub by my hair. I can feel exactly where he grabbed—a hot, stinging map of his fingers on my skull.

The masks shatter beautifully, actually. Each one was a gift. Each one delicate and carefully collected over the years. He knows this. That's why he breaks them slowly, holding each one up so I can see it before he smashes it against the wall—making eye contact. Making sure I'm watching. The wedding glasses next—crystal, catching the light as they explode.

I was watching my life become shrapnel.

He tears the phone out of the wall as he grabs my cat and anything he hasn't broken and piles it into my truck.

Left throbbing and bewildered with my Christmas present. Bright, warm, happy yellow. I loved this jacket five days ago. Now there are droplets on the sleeve—mine—catching the streetlight as I stumble down the middle of the road. The snow glows orange under the lamps. My breath comes out in clouds. Each step crunches.

Is he circling the block?

I keep walking. The yellow jacket suddenly feels thin. The cold bites through it now, or maybe that's just shock making my whole body shake.

At fourteen, I thought this was love. At sixteen, I thought I could fix him. At nineteen, I believed "I'll never drink again." At twenty, I had a loaded gun in my face, and I'm finally, *finally* understanding.

I knock on a door. The man who gave me that innocent New Year's kiss answers. It was an innocent peck from this friend of his that set him off at the stroke of midnight. He was busy at the bar and caught a glimpse that, in his distorted state, made it appear nefarious. The kiss that caused all this. Except it didn't cause anything. I know that. But my husband's rage needed a reason, needed a trigger, needed something to blame that wasn't the alcohol or the need for violence or the fact that he was always going to do this.

I wait behind a curtain for my grandmother. Watching for my own truck to come down the street. Watching for my husband to come finish what he started.

She shows up as my savior, and I spend my first free night in a warm bed in her safe haven. My body and mind are numb.

I never went back to that home I shared with him, or to him.

Finally done with the empty promises, not bothering with yet another restraining order, long before stalking was a crime, and was done.

Six weeks of marriage. A lifetime of running.

About Jennifer Pedrotti

A woman who found peace in loving her new husband, children, grandchild, and dog. After a long, successful career at a national security laboratory, I found happiness and fulfillment in retirement.

8

NEW YORK
BY BELIA PAUL

I didn't leave Davy in a blaze of courage. I didn't pack a suitcase with dignity and walk away like some empowered woman in a movie. I just didn't go home one day. That's how it happened. I passed my freeway exit and kept driving, past the off-ramp, past everything I had known for the last three years, until I found myself in front of Chris's place with nothing but the clothes I left to work in and fear, so much fear my hands shook on the wheel.

I had been with Davy for years, and it was dark in a way that made me disappear. He was charming, intense, the kind of man who looked straight through you. I learned to soften my voice, to make my opinions smaller. I learned to tiptoe. To keep the peace. He wanted me quiet, invisible, his version of safe.

But this isn't a story about Davy. Not really.

It's about what came after.

Chris was different. Not louder. Not bigger. Just calm. He didn't raise his voice or use love as leverage. He listened. After years of hiding, that steadiness felt both comforting and unfamiliar. For the first time in a long time, I wasn't being managed. I didn't have to ask permission to exist.

We moved into a house made almost entirely of glass on the Big Island. Floor-to-ceiling windows opened onto wide pastures, and at night the world went still. After years of noise — yelling, crying, emotional landmines- the quiet was unlike anything I had known. It felt unsettling and nourishing at the same time.

Chris worked during the day. I was alone with time, more time than I knew what to do with. I filled it the way I knew how: cleaning, nesting, wandering. I tried to let myself just be, but I didn't yet know how.

Chris encouraged me to use the quiet to figure out who I was and what I wanted. But I didn't know how to want anything without first asking if it was okay.

Even in calm, I defaulted to pleasing. I was still learning how to exist without being shaped.

I searched for belonging where people often do, in community, in ritual, in churches that promised answers. We tried a few. None of them felt right. Whatever I was looking for, I didn't find it there either.

And underneath it all, I was still trying. Trying to find where I belonged. Trying on different versions of myself, feeling for one that didn't smother or mask or make me itch in my skin.

I had never been to the East Coast before. Chris used his frequent flyer miles to buy our tickets. We were flying across the country to attend his youngest brother, Blaire's, wedding, a big, formal Catholic ceremony in New York. I didn't know how long it had been since he'd seen his family, but the trip felt weighted somehow.

Chris was one of seven siblings. The youngest worked on Wall Street and was marrying into a strict Irish Catholic family. Everything about the weekend carried a certain tone. Proper. Traditional. Tight-lipped.

I didn't fully understand what I was walking into, but I knew this wouldn't be the kind of wedding where we danced barefoot or toasted with mai tais.

Just before we left, I cut my hair. Not a trim, a real cut. Six or eight inches gone. I gave myself bangs, hoping to feel grown, city ready. Instead, I felt exposed. The second the scissors clicked shut, I regretted it. I boarded the flight already uncomfortable in my own skin.

Blaire and his roommates were away on a bachelor weekend, so we stayed in his Brooklyn apartment. His room felt like a preserved version of boyhood, cluttered and unquestioned. I was excited for the quiet before the formalities began, before the rules I didn't yet understand came fully into play.

We spent a day at the Jersey Shore, where the bride's family unlocked a private cabana on the beach. Everything felt ordered and exclusive in a way I didn't yet understand.

The rehearsal dinner was held at a boutique hotel in New Jersey, with soft lighting, white tablecloths, and waiters in black vests. I was lucky to sit beside Chris.

He was being pulled in every direction, family and old friends, playing the role of big brother, but somehow, I landed next to him.

Grilled New York steak was on the menu, so I ordered it. When the server asked how I wanted it cooked, I blinked. "Grilled," I said, as if he hadn't read the menu himself.

The table fell silent.

Chris leaned in and whispered, "You like it medium rare."

I felt my face flush. Mortified, I stared at my lap and nodded.

At the reception the next night, Chris was seated at the head table, and I was placed at what I came to think of as the misfit table, singles, elderly relatives, and obligatory guests.

I wore a cream dress that hugged my sun-kissed skin. I stood out. My body entered the room before I did. Men watched. Women observed. It had always been that way.

But that night, under crystal chandeliers and the clink of silverware, it felt like a spotlight I couldn't escape.

A woman, an aunt, I think, sat beside me, sipping wine and smiling sweetly. She leaned in slowly, her perfume faint, her hair too dark with dye. She touched my shoulder with her fingertips, then traced a line down my arm, not quickly, but with the careful precision you use when checking for splinters. As if I were something carved.

Her voice was soft, barely audible, like a secret meant only for me.

"Your kind is so beautiful."

I froze.

I didn't know what she meant. I only knew I had been named. I blinked at her, half-smiling, unsure how to respond. Somewhere in the back of my mind, I heard Davy's voice: " You're *kind? You mean the help?*

It felt like a slap wrapped in satin. Polite on the outside but condescending all the way through.

And I had to sit in it. Still, polite, unsure, simmering with something I didn't yet know how to name.

After the reception, we traveled upstate by train to the family property in Woodstock. The Hudson slid past the windows, green and still. I rested my head on Chris's shoulder and listened to childhood stories spill out of him. It was the most relaxed I'd seen him in days.

The family's compound in Woodstock was rustic and sprawling, filled with maple trees and winding dirt roads. But everything about it felt curated, as if even the wilderness had been edited. Everyone was arriving: siblings, partners, children, parents. The whole clan.

They had a system. Unmarried men in one house, unmarried women in another, and the official couples in the main home. Chris and I, despite living together, didn't have the paperwork to prove our legitimacy. So we were split.

That stung. We were well over a week into the trip, and I wanted his comfort, his reassurance that I was managing this okay.

I wanted him to hold me and tell me they were going to be okay with me, even if we both knew that probably wasn't true.

Instead, I felt as if I were temporary. That I didn't quite belong.

One day, while rubbing my eye, one of my contact lenses popped out, and just like that, the world went fuzzy.

I didn't want to make a fuss. I didn't want to wear my glasses either. That felt like another exposure I wasn't ready for. I pulled Chris aside. We made a few calls and somehow convinced a doctor to overnight a single lens to the middle of Woodstock. Chris paid for it.

When FedEx came crunching down the gravel driveway, the kids ran to greet it like an ice cream truck. I carried the package to the women's house, washed my hands, and carefully popped the lens in.

I breathed.

And then, maybe an hour later, I lost it again. Just rubbed my eye out of habit and poof.

I was in the kitchen when it happened. Everyone else had gone outside for a game of bocce ball, and I was crouched near the fridge, patting the floor, my heart racing. I didn't want to ask for help again. I didn't want anyone to see me frantic, needy, or undone.

And then Chris appeared.

He didn't ask what I was doing. He didn't comment. He just got down on his hands and knees beside me and started looking.

We found the lens clinging to the chair leg.

I rinsed it, slipped it back in, and went outside to join the others.

But something had shifted.

Names and identifying details are presented as remembered, not as recorded. This story reflects lived experience, not objective history.

About Belia Paul

Belia Paul is a writer, caregiver advocate, and founder of A Honu Space, a Maui based organizing and kūpuna support service that helps families navigate aging, caregiving, and life transitions. Her work is shaped by personal experiences supporting loved ones through dementia, disability, and complex family caregiving.

Her stories explore the quiet moments that shape us, especially when we feel out of place or unsure of where we belong. The story she contributed to this collection is part of a larger body of work she is developing into a future book of personal essays and short stories.

Belia lives on Maui where she continues to support caregivers and kūpuna through organizing, education, and community advocacy.

Contact: belia@ahonuspace.com   www.ahonuspace.com

9

BLUE-EYED BOY
BY MARLENA TANNER

It was an ordinary summer evening in northwestern Alberta, where the sun lingered on the horizon, delaying nightfall until well past midnight. The extended daylight made it challenging for children to adhere to their usual bedtimes, prompting mothers to hang black curtains in their rooms to simulate darkness. It was during one of these seemingly endless summer nights that a tragic incident unfolded. It irrevocably altered the course of my life, leaving me with a multitude of unanswered questions and a heavy burden of guilt that would haunt me and my family afterwards.

This is a story of survival, resilience, and fortitude. It is a harrowing tale I do not wish upon my worst enemy. It profoundly impacted two families who spent four decades grappling with the aftermath of an incomprehensible tragedy. Although these families drifted apart over time, they found a way to move forward, honoring the memory of a beautiful blue-eyed boy named Bobby. Their journey reflects a commitment to making the most of their futures while keeping his spirit alive.

I share this story to confront my trauma head-on and seek the closure I sought for so long. By naming, writing, and sharing my story, I embark on a journey of healing that addresses both my emotional and physical well-being. Speaking my truth and exposing my deepest wounds serves as a profound act of self-healing, benefiting not only me but hopefully those who have faced similar challenges. This tragedy no longer defines me; it is merely a chapter in my life that has reshaped me into the person I am today. I choose to embrace my reality and use the scars I carry to guide and inspire others.

This is the story that rocked my world…

My family lived in a townhouse on the northeast side of an oil town in Canada, located several hundred miles south of the Yukon Territory. As the eldest of four siblings, I demonstrated maturity and responsibility beyond my years.

By the age of ten, I had already taken several babysitting jobs. One family I frequently cared for had two delightful boys, Nathan, aged four, and his two-year-old brother, Bobby, both had thick brown hair and striking blue eyes. They were new to the area and lived in the same complex as my family, which allowed me to form a close bond with them. I do not recall every specific detail from those formative years, but I clearly remember the boys were exceptionally polite and well-mannered, which made my experience as a babysitter remarkably easy.

Our two-story townhouse, complete with a small grassy yard and wooden fencing for privacy, became a vibrant hub of neighborhood activity. Perhaps it was the proximity of the park just around the corner, or maybe it was simply the presence of me and my three siblings, which attracted kids of all ages. Regardless of the reason, our home was undeniably the local gathering spot. My parents were exceptional hosts, frequently organizing dinners throughout my childhood. I distinctly remember one rainy summer weekend when we chose to host Nathan and Bobby's family for dinner, adding to the lively atmosphere our home was known for. On that fateful evening, there were no grand celebrations in store; it was simply an unplanned gathering with a family still getting acquainted with the neighborhood.

After dinner, the children went to the park to run off some steam. I chose to stay home, settling in to watch a movie in our basement, a space where we kids spent countless hours building forts and playing hide-and-seek. Meanwhile, Nathan and Bobby's mom chose to stay behind to keep my mother company. Unbeknownst to me, the events that unfolded next would plunge me into utter chaos and a state of frenzy.

To this day, I remain perplexed by both fathers' decision to stay behind. I later learned they had become absorbed in a conversation in the living room, prompting my younger sister to take the children to the park instead. As I was about to settle into my movie, I heard a blood-curdling scream from upstairs. I couldn't discern whether it was my mother's scream or that of the other mother. Instinctively, I bolted up the stairs, leaving the opening credits illuminated on the screen as I sought the source of the distressing cry. Upon reaching the top of the stairs and racing down the hallway, I spotted my father entering the house, followed by Bobby's father closely behind. Bobby appeared unconscious and lifeless in his father's arms, a significant patch of hair missing from his head, yet his skull remained miraculously intact.

The chaos that ensued remains a blur in my memory. Recently, my mother recounted how the adults thought it best for the two fathers to jump into our family car and rush Bobby to the nearest hospital, fearing the ambulance would take too long. As this unfolded, the children started trickling into the house one by one. Little Nathan, innocent and confused, was unaware of the gravity of the situation. In a flurry, my mother dashed upstairs to fetch my sister's Curious George stuffed toy to comfort him, leaving me in the living room, grappling with Nathan and his mother's distress. I cannot recall if I offered her any words of comfort – what could I possibly say to a mother facing the terrifying uncertainty of her child's fate?

When my mother returned, she was composed enough to recount the events that had transpired. Both mothers were in the kitchen, busy washing and drying dishes. As light rain began to fall, my little brother decided to come inside. While glancing out the kitchen window, my mother noticed Bobby playing in a puddle in the parking lot adjacent to the sidewalk. My mom asked Bobby's mother if she wanted to bring him in as well. Her reply was simply, "He's okay. He's used to playing outside in the rain." However, just moments later, my mother glanced out the window again and witnessed Bobby being struck by our neighbor's truck.

The neighbor, who lived in the townhouse across from us, had been drinking. He unexpectedly reversed his truck out of its usual spot and into our family's parking area, something he had never done before. Normally, he would back up halfway into the parking lot before turning towards the exit, but this time he reversed all the way to the sidewalk area where Bobby was playing. In a horrifying, rapid-fire sequence of events, my mother watched as the neighbor's truck knocked Bobby down and then, in a misguided attempt to correct his path, backed up again–this time over Bobby's head. The chilling reality of the situation culminated in my mother's terrifying scream, a visceral response to the unimaginable horror she had just witnessed.

Years later, my youngest brother, who was the same age as Bobby at the time, recounted his own memories of that unforgettable day. He vividly remembered Bobby expressing a desire to play in a puddle in the parking lot, while my brother chose to go inside the house. It is astonishing to consider my brother could just as easily have been the one struck by the car instead of Bobby. His single, pivotal choice left our family intact both physically and emotionally, whereas the unintended consequences of Bobby's choice left his family physically and emotionally bereft.

Bobby was airlifted by helicopter to a city approximately 200 miles away, where advanced lifesaving technology was accessible. The days that followed felt like an eternity as we desperately waited for any updates on his condition. After two days on life support, we received the heartbreaking news of Bobby's passing, leaving us in profound shock and disbelief. It was unfathomable that such a devastating event could befall both families. We gave the other family their space to mourn as our family navigated our own grief.

A few weeks later, I was asked to care for Nathan, likely a much-needed respite for his parents. I distinctly remember him asking, "Why is my brother Bobby gone? Where did he go?" It took immense strength to hold back my tears as I struggled to offer a comforting response in that moment. As a child myself, I found it incredibly difficult to comprehend the gravity of the situation. What words could I offer to ease the pain of a four-year-old? In the end, I found solace in reassuring Nathan that Bobby was in heaven and God was watching over him.

That summer, Bobby was not the only child to tragically lose his life in our community; he was one of three young boys who died within the same month. The aftermath of such trauma left our family feeling lost and empty, prompting the need to escape the weight of our grief. A few months after Bobby's passing, we had the opportunity to move to British Columbia, taking up residence in my grandparents' former home as they transitioned to their new home, located a day's drive away. This timing proved serendipitous, as leaving Alberta became a necessary step for us, particularly for my mother, who was haunted by memories of that fateful night every time she looked out the kitchen window. Although it was difficult to say goodbye to our friends, this move gave us the fresh start we so desperately needed to begin our healing.

I struggled for many years to comprehend the reasons behind my feelings. Guilt weighed heavily on me for choosing to stay home on the night of the accident instead of joining the other children at the park. Had I been present, I am convinced I would have kept a close eye on both Bobby and my youngest brother, thereby preventing this tragedy. I often reflect on how beneficial it might have been if my parents had pursued therapy for my siblings and me. However, during that time, such practices were not common; instead, we relied on prayer and tried to move on with our lives.

Despite the passage of time, my memories of Bobby remained vivid. A doctor once told me that physical healing cannot occur without first addressing emotional wounds, a notion I initially dismissed. After enduring a relentless autoimmune disease and growing increasingly frustrated with my slow recovery, I decided to confront the emotions tied to Bobby's death and the trauma of that night. I began practicing Emotional Freedom Technique (EFT), which I had learned about several years earlier. This method involves tapping on acupressure points to stimulate the body's energy system, sending calming signals to the amygdala part of the brain and effectively reprogramming the brain's stress response to reduce both emotional distress and physical pain.

I finally worked up the courage to return to my family's townhouse in Alberta after forty years, but tears did not come when I found myself in the parking lot where our neighbor's car had tragically struck Bobby. I wandered through the complex with my husband, reminiscing about the joyful moments of my youth. As the sun began to set, we decided to leave and return the next day with a fresh perspective. The townhouse appeared the same, though it now featured additional metal fencing to contain a rottweiler. I spotted the familiar groove in the asphalt where water had once pooled, the very spot that had captivated Bobby's playful spirit. As I tapped while looking down at this impression in the road, the tears finally flowed freely as I said my final heartfelt goodbyes to him. Eventually, a sense of calm washed over me, and the tears gave way to a smile. I shared with my husband that I had finally found the closure I had long sought, or so I thought…

I recently discovered neuromuscular re-education, a therapeutic technique that retrains the brain and muscles to function in harmony. While this method is particularly beneficial for those recovering from injuries, surgeries, or neurological conditions, I learned neuromuscular re-education can also address emotional issues stemming from childhood trauma. During the session, I learned how the brain cannot tell reality from imagination. For instance, the brain is unable to distinguish between the stress caused by childhood trauma and the immediate threat of being pursued by a predatory animal.

I was encouraged to visualize my trauma through the lens of my heart rather than my mind, as the latter often influences my emotional responses. As I relaxed, an image of a beautiful blue-eyed boy surfaced, accompanied by the painful memories of his death. I found myself overwhelmed by tears, as I thought I had dealt with this specific emotional trauma. At that moment, I was asked to replace this painful image with a more uplifting one. Now, when I reflect on the emotional scars from that momentous night, I envision Bobby flying a bright-colored kite as he joyfully runs along the beach. Neuromuscular re-education allows me to connect these positive memories with Bobby, serving as a powerful reminder that he is living his best life and would not want me to wallow in sorrow. Instead, he would encourage me to wholeheartedly embrace life.

It was not long after Bobby's passing that his mother became pregnant again, giving birth to a lovely baby girl. I felt a sense of joy knowing Nathan would not have to grow up as an only child. The parents named the girl after my mother. Years later, my husband and I encountered this family and had the opportunity to meet their daughter for the first time. Although the meeting was somewhat awkward, they were incredibly kind and gracious. Unfortunately, that would be the last time I would ever see them.

As an adult, I have come to understand the reasons for this family's estrangement from us. While geographical distance played a role, I believe the memories of that tragic evening continue to haunt them, forever linking our families to the events of that night. A few years ago, we learned they relocated to British Columbia and now live across the lake from my parents. I proposed to my parents that arranging a meeting might offer a sense of closure for both families. One day, my father took the initiative to visit them, and, although they were cordial, he sensed they wanted to be left alone. This realization saddens me; however, I find solace in knowing I do not need their approval to face my emotional struggles. I have control over my own thoughts and feelings, and I am equipped with the necessary tools to manage them when they arise.

Navigating the complexities of childhood trauma is an ongoing journey, and I embrace that reality. The experiences I have endured have shaped me into the person I am today, fostering significant personal growth and emotional resilience. The healing I have achieved, both emotionally and physically, is a testament to the fortitude I have built through adversity. While the events of my childhood do not solely define me, they contribute to the rich tapestry of my existence. I have come to terms with the guilt associated with that pivotal night, recognizing that a remarkable blue-eyed boy is thriving as he was meant to. Our time on this beautiful planet is fleeting, and I believe a greater purpose awaits each of us beyond this life.

Until we cross paths again, dear little one, I wish you peace and joy as you journey toward brighter days ahead.

About Marlena Tanner

Marlena Tanner is an aspiring author who resides in Southern California. Over the past three decades, she and her husband have dedicated themselves to expanding their management consulting firm, traveling to numerous locations around the world, and raising two wonderful children.

Her initial introduction into the realm of writing came through a collaborative effort with Rapid Feline Media. Her published work can be found in a coffee table book titled, *Dear Me: Hold On – Letters to Carry Us Through the Darkest Times*. In her chapter, she offers a message of hope not only to her younger self but also to others facing similar adversities.

Marlena is currently writing a daily reflection book designed for those seeking respite from a hectic world, navigating health challenges, reconnecting with nature, and discovering their life's purpose.

Lanterns in the Dark